THE CHALLENGE OF
Space

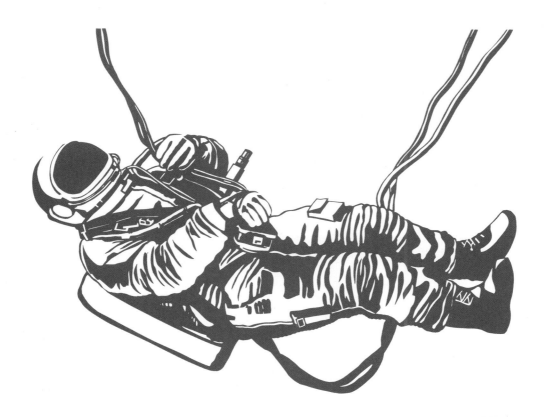

Writer: Robin Kerrod
Designer: Tri-Art
Illustrators: Derek Bunce, Jeff Burn, Wilfred Hardy,
John Harwood, John Marshall, Mike Roffe
Cover Illustrator: John Marshall
Series Editor: Christopher Tunney
Art Director: Keith Groom

LIBRARY OF CONGRESS CATALOGING IN PUBLICATION DATA

Kerrod, Robin.
The challenge of space.

(The Question and answer books)
Includes index.
SUMMARY: Surveys rockets, satellites, and space travel
in question and answer format.

1. Astronautics—Miscellanea—Juvenile literature. 2. Rockets (Aeronautics)—Miscellanea—Juvenile literature. [1. Astronautics. 2. Rockets (Aeronautics) 3. Questions and answers]
I. Bunce, Derek. II. Title.

TL793.K465   1980   629.4   C   79-64385
ISBN 0-8225-1177-0   lib. bdg.

This revised edition © 1980 by Lerner Publications Company.
Published simultaneously in Canada by J. M. Dent & Sons (Canada) Ltd.,
Don Mills, Ontario.

First edition copyright © 1978 by Sackett Publicare Ltd.

International Standard Book Number: 0-8225-1177-0
Library of Congress Catalog Card Number: 79-64385

Manufactured in the United States of America.

1 2 3 4 5 6 7 8 9 10 85 84 83 82 81 80

73124

The Question and Answer Books

THE CHALLENGE OF
Space

 Lerner Publications Company ▪ **Minneapolis**

What is space?

SPACE We live in one of the most exciting periods of history. Today we can do something people have been dreaming about for centuries—we can travel in space. We started going into space in 1961, only four years after the first artificial moon was launched. Now we can fly hundreds of thousands of miles across space to the real Moon. Yet at the beginning of this century nobody had succeeded in flying an airplane even a few hundred yards!

The Earth we live on has around it a thin layer of gases, which we call the *atmosphere*. Near the ground the atmosphere is quite thick. But it gets thinner the higher we rise above the Earth's surface. Above about 100 miles (160 km), there is hardly any atmosphere left. Then we are in space.

Where is the Earth in space?

Sun

Mars

White dwarf star

Red giant star

Moon

The Earth is one of a multitude of bodies that exist in space. Between these bodies there is nothing except a few atoms of gas and specks of dust. Earth is a planet, which travels with eight others around the Sun. The Sun is a star—the nearest star to us. Like most other stars, it is a ball of glowing gas.

How big is space?

Nearest galaxy
20,000 million years

Nearest star
500,000 years

The Sun
3 weeks

The Moon
2½ days

Earth

It is difficult to imagine how big space is. But an idea of its size can be gotten if we imagine setting out to explore it in a rocket. In our rocket, we would reach the Moon in about 2½ days, and the Sun in about 3 weeks. But it would take us over half a million years to reach even the next nearest star, and thousands of millions of years to reach the nearest galaxy.

What is it like in space?

Up in space, there is no air. So there can be no sound, because sound needs air to travel in. There can be no clouds, no rain, no snow. Space is dark. You can see things only when sunlight shines on them. In the Sun, it is very hot. Out of the Sun, it is deathly cold.

Why go into space?

Space, then, is a hostile world for us. And traveling in space is very dangerous. So why go there? One of the main reasons is that it presents a challenge to the inventive mind. It is there, waiting to be explored. And by exploring space, we find out more about how the universe is made up and how we fit into it.

GETTING INTO SPACE When people decided to explore space, they had to find a way of getting there. Many difficulties had to be faced and overcome. The main problem to be solved was how to defeat the pull of the Earth, which attracts every object to its surface. When we found a way of overcoming this pull, we were able to launch a body into space, to become an artificial moon of the Earth.

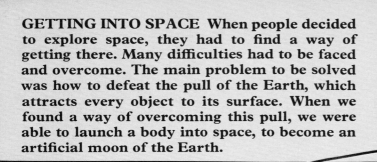

What is gravity?

We call the pull of the Earth *gravity*. Because of gravity, everything we throw or drop falls to the ground. And every falling object accelerates toward the Earth at the same rate. This means that light objects fall as quickly as heavy ones.

How does gravity affect us?

Gravity affects things profoundly. It keeps our feet firmly on the ground. It keeps the atmosphere in place. All the heavenly bodies have gravity too. It is the Moon's gravity that attracts the water in the oceans and causes the tides. The Sun's powerful gravity keeps the planets (including the Earth) circling around it in space. The bigger a body is, the greater is its gravity.

Who first discovered gravity?

The first person to realize that gravity is a basic force of the universe was Isaac Newton, one of history's most brilliant thinkers. It is said that he thought out his ideas on gravity after seeing apples fall from a tree in his garden.

How can we beat gravity?

When a shell is fired into the air from a gun, it soars upward at high speed. As it slows, it curves back to Earth because gravity pulls it. But for a while its speed defeated gravity. The faster the shell goes, the higher it soars before it falls back to Earth.

What is a satellite?

If you had a very, very powerful gun, you could fire the shell so fast that it would overcome gravity and stay up in space. To do so, it must travel at more than about 17,500 mph (28,000 kph). At this speed, it can circle around the Earth as an artificial moon, or *satellite*.

Why does it not fall down?

A satellite stays in its orbit (path) around the Earth for a long time, because there is no air or anything else to slow it down. But if it does slow down, gravity will pull it back to Earth.

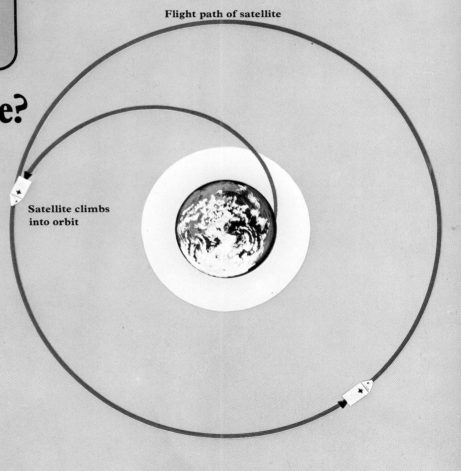

Flight path of satellite

Satellite climbs into orbit

How do rockets work?

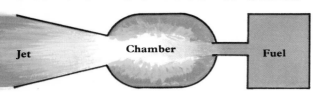

Jet   Chamber   Fuel

Rockets work by burning fuel inside a combustion chamber. This produces hot gases, which expand and shoot out of the chamber through a nozzle. They escape from the nozzle as a high-speed jet. Reaction to the backward jet creates the forward thrust.

Why can jet engines not be used in space?

Fuel

Air

Rockets can work in space because they carry the oxygen they need to burn their fuel. Jet engines cannot be used in space because they need oxygen from the air. The fuel and oxygen a rocket carries are called *propellants*.

What kinds of rockets are there?

ROCKETS IN SPACE We can cheat gravity and climb into space by launching ourselves from the Earth at about 17,000 miles (28,000 km) an hour. This speed is outside our normal experience. Even the fastest jet fighters can travel at little more than 2,000 miles (3,000 km) an hour. The ordinary engines we use on Earth are simply not powerful enough to achieve the kinds of speeds necessary for space travel. But rockets can be built that exert a thrust of over 7 million pounds (3 million kilos), powerful enough to speed spacecraft into the depths of space.

Solid fuel

Liquid oxygen

Fuel

Pumps

Combustion chamber

Exhaust gases

Exhaust gases

There are two main kinds of rockets, which are classed by the type of propellant they use. The most important kind uses liquid propellants, such as kerosene (fuel) and liquid oxygen (oxidant). The propellants are kept in huge tanks and pumped to the combustion chamber. The other main kind of rocket has a solid propellant. It is kept in a tube which also acts as the combustion chamber. Solid rockets are not as powerful as liquid ones.

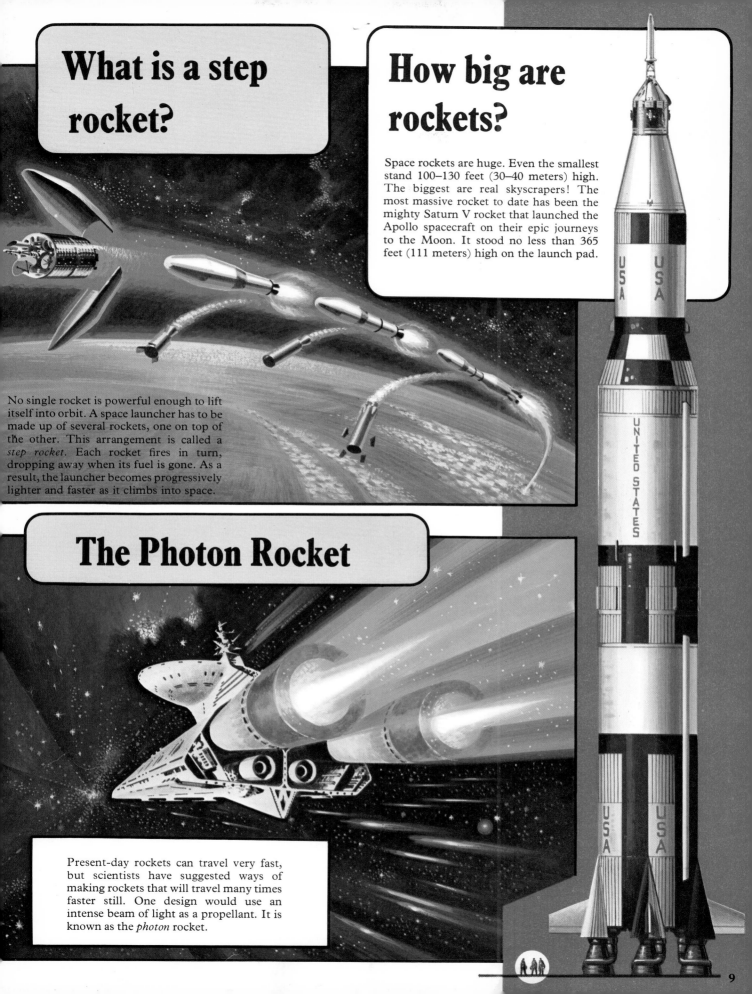

What is a step rocket?

No single rocket is powerful enough to lift itself into orbit. A space launcher has to be made up of several rockets, one on top of the other. This arrangement is called a *step rocket*. Each rocket fires in turn, dropping away when its fuel is gone. As a result, the launcher becomes progressively lighter and faster as it climbs into space.

How big are rockets?

Space rockets are huge. Even the smallest stand 100–130 feet (30–40 meters) high. The biggest are real skyscrapers! The most massive rocket to date has been the mighty Saturn V rocket that launched the Apollo spacecraft on their epic journeys to the Moon. It stood no less than 365 feet (111 meters) high on the launch pad.

The Photon Rocket

Present-day rockets can travel very fast, but scientists have suggested ways of making rockets that will travel many times faster still. One design would use an intense beam of light as a propellant. It is known as the *photon* rocket.

9

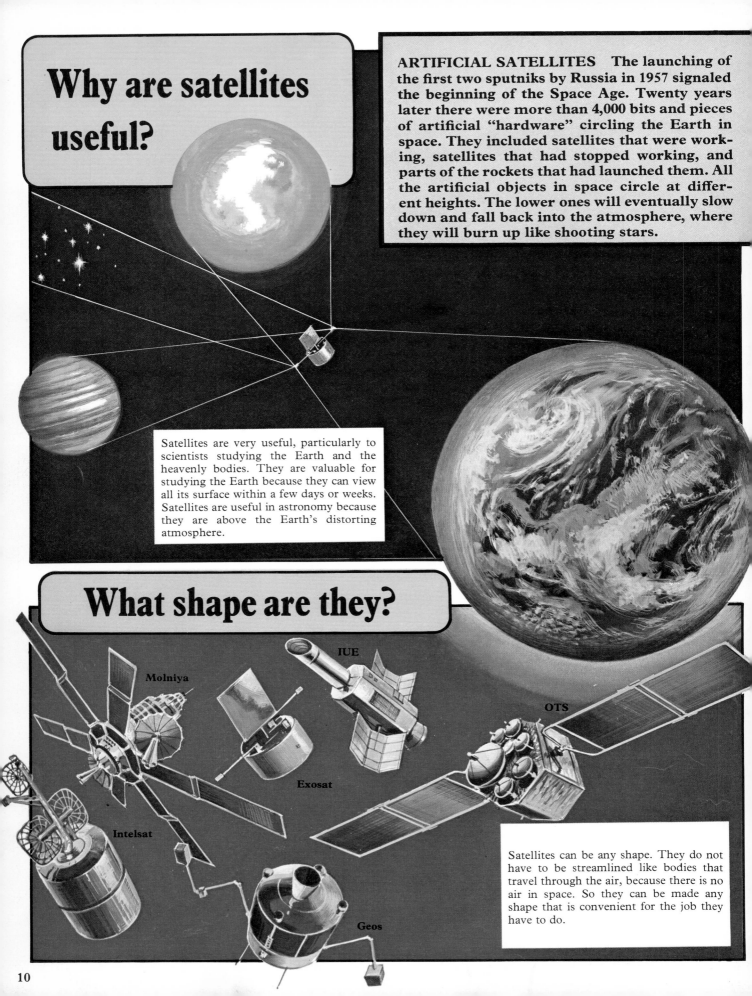

Why are satellites useful?

ARTIFICIAL SATELLITES The launching of the first two sputniks by Russia in 1957 signaled the beginning of the Space Age. Twenty years later there were more than 4,000 bits and pieces of artificial "hardware" circling the Earth in space. They included satellites that were working, satellites that had stopped working, and parts of the rockets that had launched them. All the artificial objects in space circle at different heights. The lower ones will eventually slow down and fall back into the atmosphere, where they will burn up like shooting stars.

Satellites are very useful, particularly to scientists studying the Earth and the heavenly bodies. They are valuable for studying the Earth because they can view all its surface within a few days or weeks. Satellites are useful in astronomy because they are above the Earth's distorting atmosphere.

What shape are they?

Molniya

IUE

OTS

Exosat

Intelsat

Geos

Satellites can be any shape. They do not have to be streamlined like bodies that travel through the air, because there is no air in space. So they can be made any shape that is convenient for the job they have to do.

What powers them?

Early satellites used ordinary batteries to provide electricity for their instruments. But most modern satellites use solar cells. These cells are made of wafers of silicon. These produce electricity when sunlight falls on them.

What are they like inside?

Scientific instrument

Guidance unit

Upper platform

Satellites differ inside, depending on their purpose. But they are all made up of several units that perform different functions. There will, for example, be an instrument unit, which will carry a variety of instruments, a power unit, and a communications unit.

Solar cells (power unit)

Upper body structure

Cooling system

Main platform (includes communication and control units)

Propellant tanks

Rocket motor

How do we keep track of them?

Space scientists keep track of satellites by means of radio and radar. They listen in to radio beams the satellites transmit, or bounce radio beams off them (radar), using large dish antennas.

SATELLITES AT WORK Satellites have already proved themselves very useful for many purposes, and their use will grow in the years ahead. They have, for example, brought about a revolution in communications. They have made it possible to transmit live television programs between countries on opposite sides of the world. Satellites have also helped weather forecasters with forecasting, and astronomers to see the universe more clearly.

What do weather satellites tell us?

How do communications satellites work?

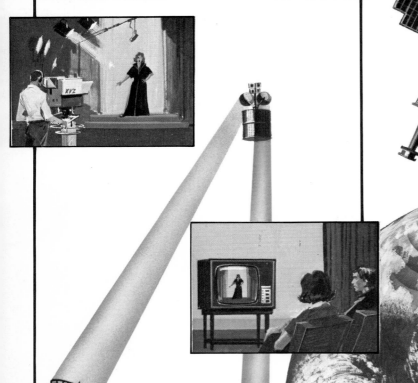

Communications satellites contain powerful amplifiers. They receive a radio beam from one ground station, strengthen it, and then beam it back down to another. Many are in stationary orbits 22,300 miles (35,900 km) above the Earth. From Earth, they appear to be fixed in the sky.

Weather satellites are equipped with cameras to take pictures of the cloud formations in the atmosphere. They also carry instruments to sense what conditions are like there. As they circle around the Earth, they provide information about the global weather scene, which makes weather forecasting much easier.

Have astronomy satellites made any discoveries?

Can satellites be used for mapping?

Astronomy satellites have made some very interesting discoveries. They have discovered peculiar X-ray stars, for example, that give off their energy in short, rapid bursts. They have found evidence of mysterious bodies called *black holes* that swallow up all matter.

Satellites have proved very useful in cartography (map-making). Photographs taken from space show the Earth's surface very clearly, and enable maps to be made with great accuracy. Using high magnification, even city streets can be made out. Ocean currents and depths are also often visible.

What else can they be used for?

The photographs and images taken by satellites provide information about rock formations, vegetation, water resources, and many other things. Satellites can also act as radio beacons for navigation and as platforms to collect information.

How do people live in a satellite?

Air freshening units

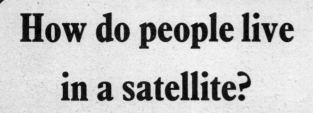

Manned rockets have a life-support system to keep astronauts alive in space. It provides them with an atmosphere that contains oxygen to breathe, and that is not too hot or cold, or too humid. Carbon dioxide and smells are removed to keep the air fresh.

What is Soyuz?

SATELLITES THAT CARRY PEOPLE The most exciting form of space travel is manned flight. More and more human beings are venturing into the alien, airless world of space. They have already landed on the Moon, and in the next century may venture to the planets. Most manned flights, however, have been flights into orbit in spacecraft that became satellites. Manned satellites are much bigger and more complicated than other satellites. Not only do they have to carry people into space, but they have to keep them alive while they are there. And they have to return them safely to Earth.

What is a heat shield?

The part of the spacecraft that carries the astronauts back to Earth re-enters the atmosphere at a tremendous speed. To keep it from burning up by friction with the air, it has to be covered with a plastic coating called a *heat shield*. This coating boils and burns, but keeps the spacecraft cool.

Descent module

Instrument module

Orbital module

Solar panel

Soyuz is the chief manned spacecraft of Russia. Its main use today is to ferry cosmonauts to and from their space station Salyut. It measures about 25 feet (7.5 meters) long and 9 feet (2.7 meters) across at its widest point.

What was Apollo?

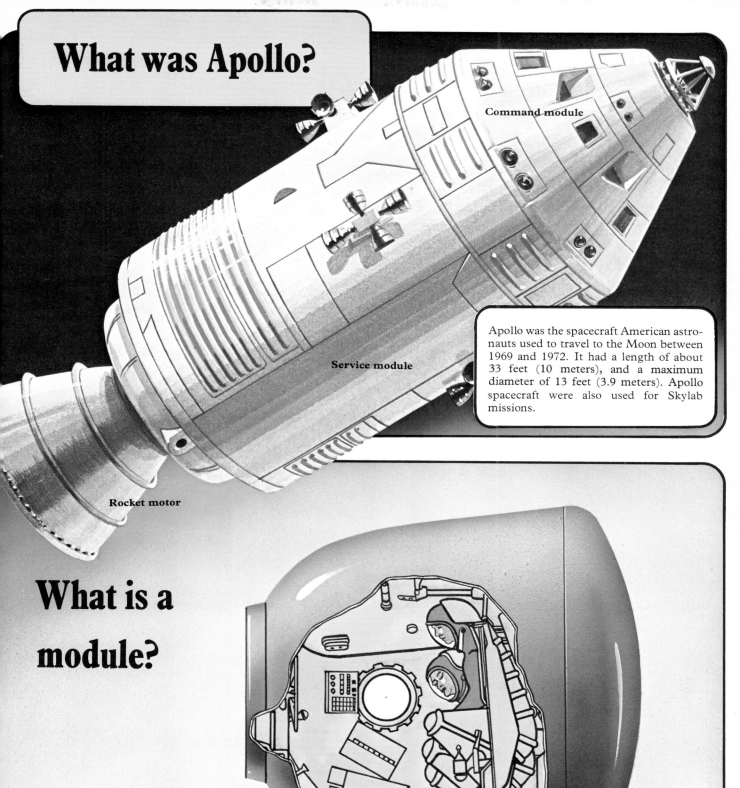

Command module

Service module

Rocket motor

Apollo was the spacecraft American astronauts used to travel to the Moon between 1969 and 1972. It had a length of about 33 feet (10 meters), and a maximum diameter of 13 feet (3.9 meters). Apollo spacecraft were also used for Skylab missions.

What is a module?

Like ordinary satellites, manned spacecraft are built with a number of units, or *modules*. One is the crew or command module, which carries the astronauts. Another is the service or equipment module, which carries such things as fuel, power, and communications equipment, and rocket motors. Only the crew module returns to Earth.

Soyuz descent module

FROM LAUNCH TO LANDING Organizing a manned spaceflight is a long and very expensive business. Great care is taken at every stage to ensure that all the equipment and systems in the rocket are working perfectly, and that there are no problems that might put the astronauts in more danger. All essential parts and systems are tested while the rocket is being assembled. After assembly it is "rolled out" of its hangar and transported to the launch pad.

What happens on the launch pad?

Next to the rocket on the launch pad is the tall service tower or *gantry*. Engineers use it to reach the assembled rocket. A few hours before departure, the rocket is fuelled. Then the astronauts climb into their cabin and prepare for blast-off.

Can the crew escape if necessary?

The crew module of a manned spacecraft is always located at the top of the rocket. A separate small rocket is attached to it. This, the escape rocket, is fired in an emergency to lift the crew module clear from the rest of the launching vehicle. The crew can then parachute to safety.

What are G-forces?

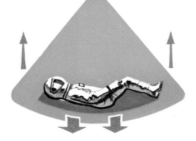

G-forces are the forces astronauts experience when their rocket accelerates. They are three or four times stronger than the downward pull we all experience because of the Earth's gravity (G). Passengers in an elevator experience slight G-forces when they move upwards.

How do spacecraft descend from orbit?

First, the astronauts maneuver their craft so that its rocket motor is pointing forward. Then they fire the motor. This slows their craft down so that it drops from orbit. Then the astronauts detach their module from the rest of the craft. Their descent module re-enters the atmosphere and starts to slow down.

How do spacecraft land?

The drag of the atmosphere brakes the descent module a great deal. Then parachutes open to slow it down further. Soyuz craft always come down on land. Apollo craft have always splashed down at sea.

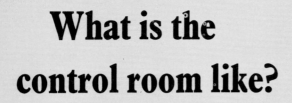

What is the control room like?

MISSION CONTROL Manned space launchings have been taking place since 1961, but all aspects of space travel are still very dangerous. Every space launching is the result of many months of detailed planning by a large team of scientists and engineers. During the actual space flight, a team of people at mission control are responsible for the successful operation of the launching rocket and the spacecraft. They are also responsible for the safety of those who are being carried into space.

Who is in charge?

In overall charge of the flight is the flight director. He keeps an eye on all the many different aspects of the mission, and also receives reports from other specialists. He makes all the decisions that affect flight operations.

This view of the Houston control center became familiar to television viewers during the Apollo Moon missions. Groups of controllers sit at control desks, or *consoles*, and follow every stage of the flight. They watch instruments and television screens linked by radio with the distant spacecraft.

Who are the other main controllers?

One controller, known as *Capcon*, is in continuous voice contact with the astronauts in the spacecraft. This controller is usually an astronaut, and knows exactly what it is like in space.

Another controller watches the flight path of the spacecraft to ensure that it is accurate. The exact position of the craft must always be known, otherwise the mission becomes very dangerous.

A third controller keeps a check on the mass of data (information) that comes from the many systems in the spacecraft. It indicates whether the systems are operating as they should.

What goes on behind the scenes?

The people sitting at the consoles in the mission control center are really the "tip of the iceberg." They are in contact with other experts who advise them on problems they can't deal with. These experts can be shown any of the pictures or data mission control receives.

Where are the U.S. tracking stations?

America's Spaceflight Tracking and Data Network (STDN) provides the vital link between mission control and the astronauts. It has stations spaced around the Earth to ensure continuous communication.

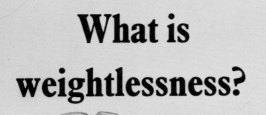

What is weightlessness?

LIVING IN ORBIT (1) Traveling in space is a strange experience for human beings, who are used to living with their feet planted firmly on the ground by gravity. But in orbit there is no gravity. This creates strange problems, as we shall see. Up in space, astronauts and cosmonauts have to work very hard, keeping themselves and their spacecraft fit, and carrying out various experiments. And, always, at the back of their minds lurks the fear that something could go wrong—for they are in an alien world.

In orbit, objects do not have any weight, because there is no effective gravity. Everything is "falling around the Earth" in the same way. This condition is known as *weightlessness*. It enables astronauts to float around and perform incredible feats of gymnastics.

What problems does it cause?

But weightlessness does cause problems. You cannot walk because there is nothing to keep your feet on the floor. Nothing stays where you put it. You cannot sit down to an ordinary meal at a table, because chairs, table, plates, and food just float away! There is no "up" or "down" in space.

How do astronauts:

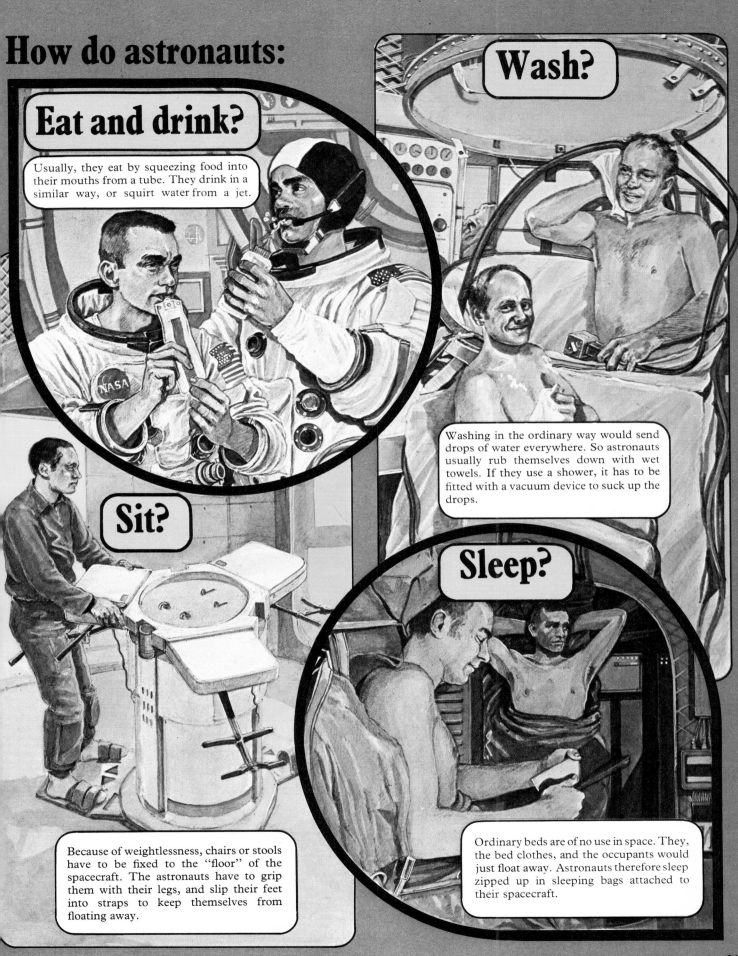

Eat and drink?

Usually, they eat by squeezing food into their mouths from a tube. They drink in a similar way, or squirt water from a jet.

Wash?

Washing in the ordinary way would send drops of water everywhere. So astronauts usually rub themselves down with wet towels. If they use a shower, it has to be fitted with a vacuum device to suck up the drops.

Sit?

Because of weightlessness, chairs or stools have to be fixed to the "floor" of the spacecraft. The astronauts have to grip them with their legs, and slip their feet into straps to keep themselves from floating away.

Sleep?

Ordinary beds are of no use in space. They, the bed clothes, and the occupants would just float away. Astronauts therefore sleep zipped up in sleeping bags attached to their spacecraft.

Is weightlessness harmful?

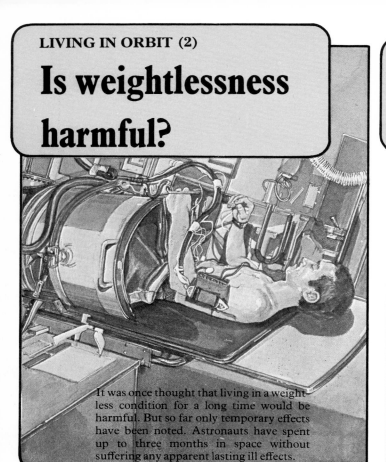

It was once thought that living in a weightless condition for a long time would be harmful. But so far only temporary effects have been noted. Astronauts have spent up to three months in space without suffering any apparent lasting ill effects.

Is it difficult to keep fit in space?

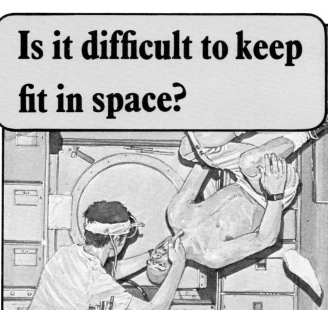

To prevent harm to their bodies, astronauts must have regular exercise while they are in orbit. Otherwise, their muscles would tend to waste away. They usually exercise in special elastic suits and on cycling machines.

What experiments do astronauts carry out?

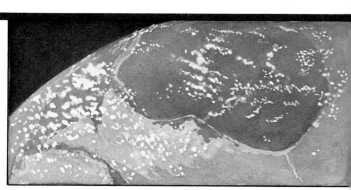

Astronauts carry out many kinds of experiments in space. They experiment with living things to see how they are affected by weightlessness. They study how crystals grow when weightless. They use instruments to photograph and study the Earth, the Sun, and other stars.

What is a space walk?

Sometimes, it is necessary for the astronauts to leave their craft in space in order to carry out repairs or to collect film from an outside camera. They then perform a space walk, or EVA (extra-vehicular activity). For this, they must wear a spacesuit to give them oxygen to breathe and to protect them from other dangers.

What is a spacesuit like?

A spacesuit is a garment that provides the astronaut with an atmosphere similar to the atmosphere on Earth. It is made up of several layers. Near the skin, the astronaut wears a water-cooled garment to prevent overheating. Over that, is a tough pressure suit, which is supplied with oxygen. Above that, is a thick oversuit and helmet, which protect the astronaut from space particles and radiation.

THE ASTRONAUTS People in the western world call them astronauts (star travelers). The Russians call them cosmonauts (space travelers). They are the brave, skilled people who travel in space, pioneers of the new Space Age. In space, they have to adapt to a new kind of existence where dangers are ever-present. It is really surprising that by 1978 only seven astronauts—four Russian and three American—had been killed in 17 years of space exploration.

What kind of people become astronauts?

Most early astronauts were highly skilled pilots, whose lightning-quick reactions enabled them to handle high-speed jets and rocket planes. But now many astronauts are scientists and engineers, skilled in their field but not in flying.

How do they train for space flights?

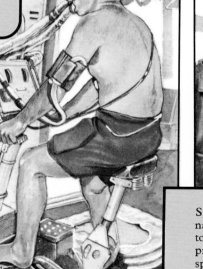

Space flights are very complicated. Astronauts have to train for a long time in order to learn all the necessary skills. They practice flight procedures in dummy spacecraft, or *simulators*. They rehearse experiments, and go to lectures.

Can they train for weightlessness?

Astronauts can gain some experience of weightlessness on Earth. One way is to travel in a plane that flies in a tight arc. Another is to swim in a water tank. They are weighted so that they neither rise nor fall and are close to being weightless.

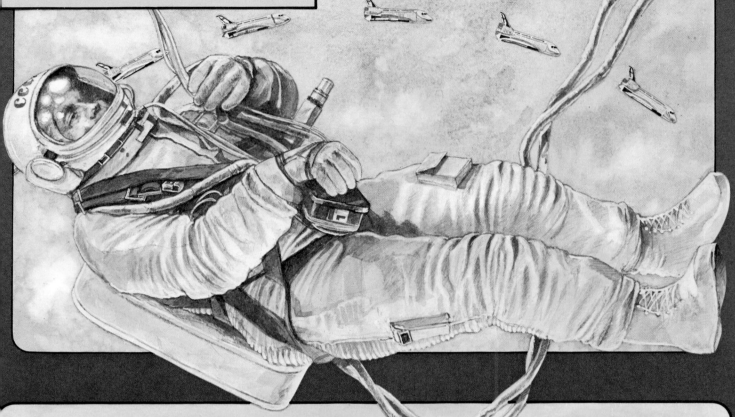

Who was the first:

Man in space?

The Russian cosmonaut Yuri Gagarin. He was launched into space on April 12, 1961, and made one orbit of the Earth in a Vostok spacecraft. He was born in Gzhatsk, west of Moscow, and was a major in the Soviet air force. Gagarin was killed in a jet crash seven years later.

American in space?

The American astronaut John Glenn. He made three orbits of the Earth in a Mercury spacecraft on February 20, 1962. He was the third man in orbit, being preceded by Yuri Gagarin and Herman Titov (17 orbits) in the previous year. He was born in Cambridge, Ohio.

Woman in space?

The Russian cosmonaut Valentina Tereshkova. Launched on June 16, 1963, she remained in orbit for three days. A few months after her return, she married fellow-cosmonaut Andrian Nikolayev. The following summer, she gave birth to the first "space baby."

What are the main parts of the shuttle?

The shuttle consists of three main parts. The crew live and work in the *orbiter*, a craft that looks much like a modern delta-winged jet airliner. This rides into space on a huge *tank*, which carries its fuel. Twin *booster rockets* are attached to the tank at take-off.

THE SPACE SHUTTLE In the past, all space launchings have been made using huge step rockets. From the 1980's on, most American space launches will be made with a new type of spacecraft—the space shuttle. It is given this name because it shuttles back and forth between Earth and space. Unlike the step rocket, which can be used only once, the shuttle can be used over and over again. This will make space launchings much cheaper. The shuttle is also big enough to carry larger crews into space than was possible before.

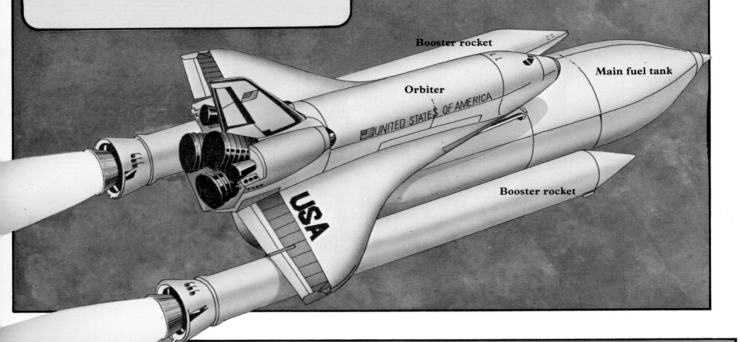

Booster rocket

Orbiter

Main fuel tank

UNITED STATES OF AMERICA

USA

Booster rocket

What is special about the shuttle?

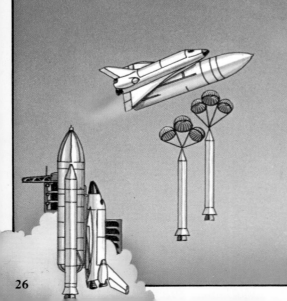

The shuttle is special because most of its parts can be used again. The orbiter's engines and the booster rockets fire to lift the shuttle off the ground. Then the boosters fall away, and parachute to the ground to be recovered. The orbiter continues into orbit, dropping the fuel tank when it is empty. After its mission, it returns to Earth.

What can it do in orbit?

73124

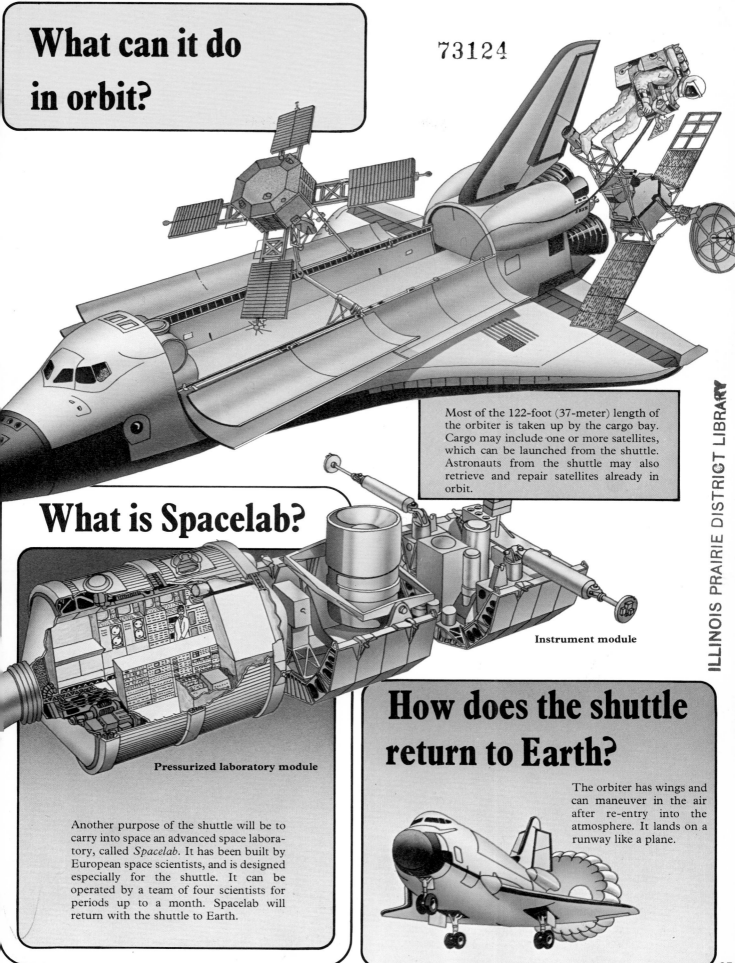

Most of the 122-foot (37-meter) length of the orbiter is taken up by the cargo bay. Cargo may include one or more satellites, which can be launched from the shuttle. Astronauts from the shuttle may also retrieve and repair satellites already in orbit.

What is Spacelab?

Pressurized laboratory module

Instrument module

Another purpose of the shuttle will be to carry into space an advanced space laboratory, called *Spacelab*. It has been built by European space scientists, and is designed especially for the shuttle. It can be operated by a team of four scientists for periods up to a month. Spacelab will return with the shuttle to Earth.

How does the shuttle return to Earth?

The orbiter has wings and can maneuver in the air after re-entry into the atmosphere. It lands on a runway like a plane.

What was Skylab?

SPACE STATIONS   Ordinary manned spacecraft do not stay in space for long periods. They are not big enough to give the astronauts comfortable living space, or to carry sufficient provisions. For long missions, much larger space stations are required. By the end of the century, very large ones will be built. They will be permanently occupied by scientists. Experimental space stations, such as the American Skylab and the Russian Salyut, have already paved the way.

Solar telescopes

Solar cells

Skylab was a space station built from Apollo rocket parts. It was launched in 1973, and was visited over a period of eight months by three three-man teams of astronauts. They were ferried to it by Apollo spacecraft. The main part of Skylab was a large cylinder, which housed the crew. The whole cluster measured 118 feet (36 meters) long.

Solar cells

Orbital workshop

What was it like inside Skylab?

This picture shows the main living quarters in Skylab, taken by a rotating camera. They consisted of the wardroom, where the crew ate and relaxed; a toilet compartment; a sleep compartment; and an experiment compartment. Note the mesh floor.

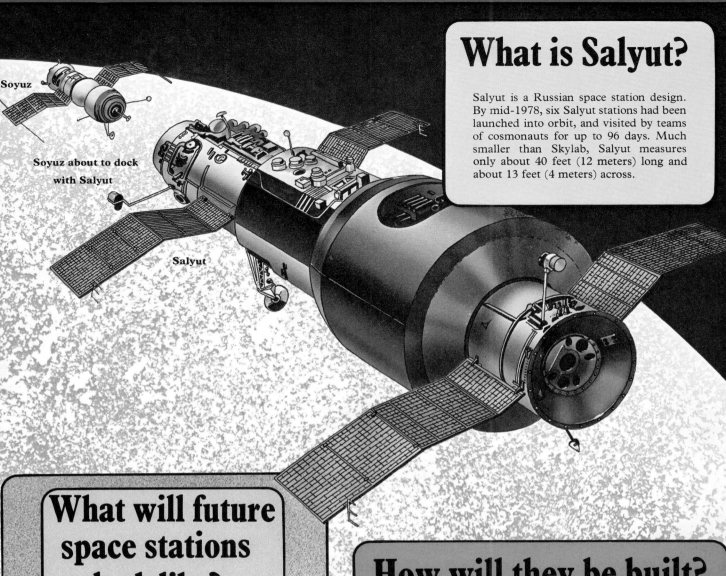

Soyuz

Soyuz about to dock
with Salyut

Salyut

What is Salyut?

Salyut is a Russian space station design. By mid-1978, six Salyut stations had been launched into orbit, and visited by teams of cosmonauts for up to 96 days. Much smaller than Skylab, Salyut measures only about 40 feet (12 meters) long and about 13 feet (4 meters) across.

What will future space stations look like?

In the future, space stations will be much bigger than either Salyut or Skylab. They will probably be built out of large cylinders joined together. They may look like this. The side units will probably be laboratories devoted to various sciences, such as biology and physics.

How will they be built?

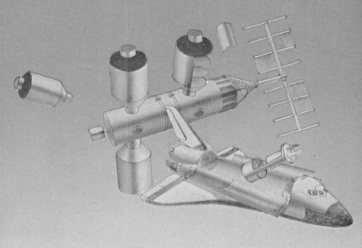

The separate sections of tomorrow's space stations will be ferried into orbit by space shuttles or larger craft. In orbit, the sections will be joined together by teams of skilled space engineers.

Steps into Space

Early science-fiction writers proposed other methods of traveling through space. The French writer Jules Verne imagined this "moon train," which was designed to be fired from a huge cannon. Note the smoke coming from the smoke stack.

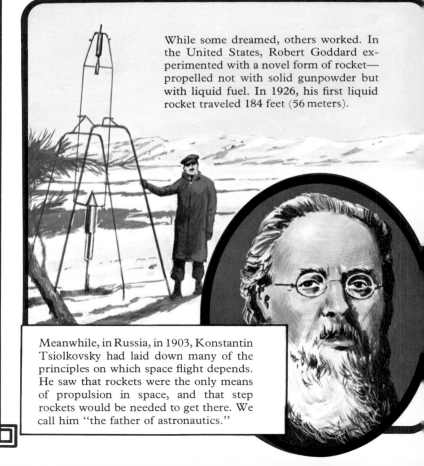

While some dreamed, others worked. In the United States, Robert Goddard experimented with a novel form of rocket—propelled not with solid gunpowder but with liquid fuel. In 1926, his first liquid rocket traveled 184 feet (56 meters).

The most important step in the history of space travel was the invention of the rocket. This followed the invention of gunpowder, the first rocket propellant, in about A.D. 900. Both inventions were made by the Chinese. The Chinese may have been using rockets in warfare at least as early as 1232.

Meanwhile, in Russia, in 1903, Konstantin Tsiolkovsky had laid down many of the principles on which space flight depends. He saw that rockets were the only means of propulsion in space, and that step rockets would be needed to get there. We call him "the father of astronautics."

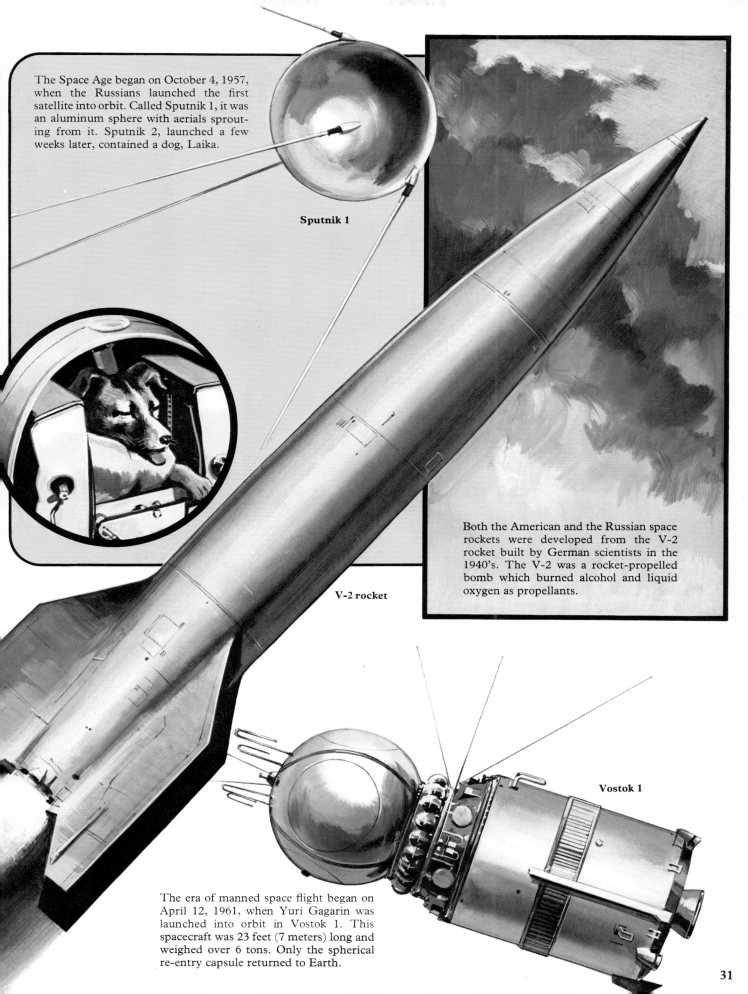

The Space Age began on October 4, 1957, when the Russians launched the first satellite into orbit. Called Sputnik 1, it was an aluminum sphere with aerials sprouting from it. Sputnik 2, launched a few weeks later, contained a dog, Laika.

Sputnik 1

Both the American and the Russian space rockets were developed from the V-2 rocket built by German scientists in the 1940's. The V-2 was a rocket-propelled bomb which burned alcohol and liquid oxygen as propellants.

V-2 rocket

Vostok 1

The era of manned space flight began on April 12, 1961, when Yuri Gagarin was launched into orbit in Vostok 1. This spacecraft was 23 feet (7 meters) long and weighed over 6 tons. Only the spherical re-entry capsule returned to Earth.

A-Z of Space Travel

A

abort Cancel or cut short a space flight.

acceleration A rate of increase of speed. In space flight, accelerations are often expressed in terms of *g*—the acceleration due to Earth's gravity. This is the acceleration anything experiences on Earth when it is dropped.

aerial An antenna.

aerospace This comes from a combination of the words *aeronautics* and *space*. It refers to flight through the Earth's atmosphere and through space.

antenna A metal rod or dish that sends out or receives radio signals.

apogee When a satellite is circling around the Earth, it is at apogee when it is at the most distant point of its orbit.

artificial gravity A kind of gravity which is created in space by rotating a spacecraft. Objects inside the spacecraft are flung outwards by centrifugal force. This imitates the pull of gravity.

artificial satellite An artificial object that orbits the Earth in space. Usually just called *satellite*.

astronautics The science of space travel. It literally means something like *traveling to the stars*. An astronaut is a space traveler.

atmosphere The layer of air around the Earth, or more generally the layer of gases around any heavenly body.

attitude The position of a spacecraft in space in relation to something else, for example, the Earth's horizon.

B

backup An item kept ready to replace another. For example, each team of astronauts which trains for a space mission has a backup team to take over if they fall ill.

blackout Temporary unconsciousness which pilots and astronauts may experience. It occurs, for example, when pilots pull out of a high-speed dive or when astronauts are suddenly accelerated. The abrupt change of speed or direction can cause blood to drain from the head. The brain is deprived of oxygen, causing faintness.

booster The first stage of a launching rocket; or a separate rocket that is attached to the main launching rocket and fires first.

burn The period of firing of a rocket.

C

capsule A term for the small pressurized cabins in which the early astronauts were sent into space.

centrifugal force A force that is caused by rotation. When you whirl a stone on a piece of string around your head, centrifugal force is the force you feel trying to pull the stone away.

centrifuge A machine used to train astronauts. They are whirled round and round quickly in the machine and experience strong centrifugal forces. These forces are similar to those they will experience in space flights.

console A control panel or desk.

cosmic rays Rays that bombard the Earth from outer space. They could be dangerous to astronauts over long periods.

cosmonaut The Russian term for *astronaut*.

countdown The counting down of time before a space flight, ending when the rocket takes off. During countdown the rocket is made ready, is filled with fuel, and is checked and double checked, item by item. If any defect is found, the countdown is halted, or *held*, until the trouble has been fixed. Then it resumes.

D

debug Find and cure any troubles or mistakes in equipment or systems.

destruct Destroying a launching rocket after lift-off. This may be necessary when the rocket's engines or systems become faulty, and it strays off course.

docking Joining two spacecraft together in space.

E

ellipse An oval shape. The orbits of satellites have the shape of an ellipse. They are termed *elliptical orbits*.

escape velocity The speed a body must have to escape from another body's gravity. To escape from the Earth's gravity, a spacecraft must have a speed of over 25,000 mph (40,000 kph).

exobiology The study of living things that may exist elsewhere in space.

extraterrestrial intelligence (ETI) Intelligent beings that may live elsewhere in space.

G

g The acceleration a body experiences when it is dropped; caused by the pull of the Earth, or *gravity*.

g-forces Forces astronauts feel when they are suddenly accelerated or slowed down. Accelerations in space flight can be five or six times stronger than *g*, the acceleration due to gravity.

gantry A steel tower positioned alongside a rocket on the launch pad. It enables engineers to reach all parts of the rocket for fueling and checking.

gravity The pull the Earth has on any body on its surface or near it in space. All heavenly bodies have gravity.

H

heat shield A coating of plastic material on a spacecraft. It helps to protect astronauts from the heat of re-entry.

hold Time during a countdown when the countdown is halted—for example, after a fault has been found.

L

launch pad The platform from which a rocket is launched.

launch vehicle A launching rocket.

launch window A period of time during which a rocket can be launched to achieve its desired orbit.

lift-off The moment when a rocket rises from the launch pad.

lox Liquid oxygen, which is used as a rocket fuel.

M

malfunction A fault.

mock-up A full-scale model of, for

example, a spacecraft. Designers use mock-ups to test their ideas. Astronauts use them to practise.

module A section of a spacecraft, such as a descent module.

multistage rocket A rocket consisting of several stages, or separate rockets, joined together.

N

nose cone The shaped cover at the front end of a rocket. It protects the spacecraft inside on its flight through the atmosphere during launching.

nozzle The part of a rocket engine through which the hot gases escape as a jet.

O

orbit The path of a satellite around the Earth, or of any heavenly body around another.

orbital period The time it takes a satellite to complete one orbit around the Earth. It varies according to the height of the satellite. At about 100 miles (160 km) high, the orbital period is about 90 minutes.

orbital velocity The speed of a satellite in orbit. It varies according to the height of the satellite. At a height of about 100 miles (160 km), the orbital velocity is about 17,500 mph (28,000 kph).

oxidant The part of a rocket propellant that provides oxygen.

P

payload The object a rocket carries into space—a satellite, spacecraft, or space probe.

perigee When a satellite is circling the Earth, it is at perigee when it is at the closest point of its orbit.

pressurized Filled with air under pressure. Manned spacecraft and spacesuits are pressurized to keep the astronauts alive when they travel in space.

probe A spacecraft sent deep into space to observe or record information about the other heavenly bodies.

propellant The material which is burned in a rocket engine to provide the hot gases that propel the rocket. The material may be liquid or solid.

R

re-entry The return of a spacecraft into the Earth's atmosphere after a space flight. During re-entry the friction (rubbing) of the air causes the spacecraft to heat up. It must therefore have a heat shield to protect it.

rendezvous The meeting in space of two spacecraft.

retro-rocket A rocket which is fired frontward in order to slow down a spacecraft. Retro-rockets are fired to bring down a spacecraft from orbit or to slow it down just before landing.

rocket An engine or motor that carries its own fuel and oxygen, which it burns to provide a jet of gases.

S

satellite A manufactured object that circles the Earth in space. We should properly call it an *artificial satellite*. In astronomy a satellite is a small body that circles around a planet. The Moon is the Earth's satellite.

simulator One of the machines astronauts train on. It is a full-size replica of, for example, a spacecraft which behaves like, or *simulates*, the real thing.

space medicine A branch of medicine dealing with the health of human beings traveling in space.

spacesuit A suit astronauts must wear when they go outside their spacecraft in space. It protects them, and provides them with air to breathe.

splashdown The moment when a spacecraft touches down at sea after a space flight.

sputnik The Russian term for a satellite.

stage One of the rocket sections of a multistage rocket, or step rocket.

stationary orbit An orbit in which a satellite appears to be stationary or fixed in the sky when viewed from the Earth. This happens at a height of about 22,300 miles (35,900 km).

step rocket Another term for a multistage rocket.

T

telemetry Measuring things from a distance. This is how scientists get information about space. They send up spacecraft fitted with instruments, which record the information on tape recorders and then radio it back to Earth.

trajectory The flight path of a body. It is often used to mean *orbit*.

U

umbilical The tube which carries oxygen, electricity, and water to an astronaut's spacesuit.

V

vacuum Where there is no air. Space is as near to a vacuum as possible.

W

weightlessness A condition astronauts experience in orbit, when their bodies appear to have no weight.

Z

zero-g A no-gravity condition; in other words, weightlessness.

Famous Rockets and Satellites

Apollo American manned spacecraft. Housing a three-man crew, Apollo took astronauts to the Moon. The first Moon landing (Apollo 11) took place on July 20, 1969. The first manned flight (in orbit) took place on October 11, 1968. Apollo was also used to ferry astronauts to and from the Skylab space station in 1973–74, and in the first international space link-up with a Russian Soyuz crew, in 1975.

Ariel Scientific satellites designed by British space engineers and launched by the United States.

Atlas American rockets used to launch Mercury spacecraft. They burned kerosene and liquid oxygen as propellants.

Cosmos Russian scientific satellites.

Echo A huge balloon which was launched as the first communications satellite, in 1960.

ERTS Stands for Earth Resources Technology Satellite. The first was launched in 1972. Now renamed Landsat.

Explorer American scientific satellites. The first one was America's first satellite (launched January 31, 1958). It made the first scientific discovery of the Space Age— of the powerful belts of radiation we now call the Van Allen belts.

Gemini American two-manned spacecraft, named after the zodiacal constellation Gemini, the Twins. The first manned Gemini flight (Gemini 3) took place on March 23, 1965. There were nine in all.

Intelsat International communications satellites. Intelsat IV and IVa satellites relay television and telephone signals between the continents from stationary orbits over the Atlantic, Pacific, and Indian Oceans.

Landsat Formerly ERTS. Earth survey satellites that photograph the Earth from space. Their photographs reveal a great deal about the Earth's resources and land mass.

Mercury American one-man spacecraft. Mercury 3 performed a manned orbital flight on May 5, 1961. John Glenn in Mercury 6 (called Friendship 7) became the first American in orbit on May 24, 1962.

Meteor Russian weather satellites.

Molniya Russian communications satellites.

Nimbus American weather satellites.

OAO Stands for Orbiting Astronomical Observatory. OAO Copernicus is famous as the first to detect the presence of a black hole.

Orbita The Russian satellite communications network.

Saturn American rockets used in their Apollo Moon landing project; also used for the later Skylab launchings. Saturn IB was a two-stage vehicle burning kerosene and liquid oxygen for the first stage and liquid hydrogen and liquid oxygen as the second stage. Saturn V, the biggest rocket ever, stood 365 feet (111 meters) high and had three stages. The first stage burned kerosene, the other stages liquid hydrogen, all with liquid oxygen. Its take-off thrust was some 7 million pounds (3 million kilos).

Soyuz The main Russian manned spacecraft. It first flew on April 23, 1967. That flight resulted in the death of its cosmonaut, Vladimir Komarov, when the landing parachute failed. In 1978 two Soyuz craft docked with Salyut 6 space station to make the first ever triple space link-up.

Sputnik Russian word for *satellite*. But most people think of Sputnik as the first Earth-orbiting satellite (October 4, 1957). It remained in orbit for 92 days. The second Sputnik, launched on November 2 of the same year, contained the first space traveler, a dog named *Laika*.

Telstar The first active communications satellite, which went into orbit in 1961.

Titan Launching rocket for America's Gemini flights. A two-stage vehicle, it had nitrogen tetroxide and Aerozine as propellants for both stages.

V2 Rocket bombs developed by the Germans in World War II. Called *Vergeltungswaffe zwei* (vengeance weapon two), it was first successfully tested in 1942, at Peenemünde in the Baltic, and used in the war in 1944.

Voshkod Early Russian manned spacecraft. The word means *sunrise*. Voshkod 1 was the first craft to take three men into space together, on October 12, 1964. Cosmonaut Aleksei Leonov in Voshkod 2 (March 18, 1965) became the first man to walk in space.

Vostok The first Russian manned spacecraft. Yuri Gagarin became the first man in orbit on April 12, 1961, in Vostok 1. *Vostok* means *east*. Six Vostok flights took place in all, the last on June 16, 1963. This carried the first woman into space— Valentina Tereshkova.

Index

Lerner Publications Company
241 First Avenue North, Minneapolis, Minnesota 55401